BUILDING
A SUCCESSFUL
WEB APP

A BUSINESSPERSON'S GUIDE
TO MAKING WEBSITES DO MORE

PAUL J. SCOTT

Cover design by Brian Halley
Book design by Nikki Ward, Morrison Alley Design

First Printing 2016

ISBN 978-0-9966874-1-6

Building A Successful Web App

Table of Contents

Introduction

Introduction

What if your website could do more? What if, instead of just displaying basic information about your organization and its products or services, it could automate key tasks, generate leads that your sales team could follow up on, or fix customer service headaches automatically without a single phone call? What if it could make employee scheduling and management a snap, or even serve as the core framework to your new web-based startup?

To most of the people I meet with for the first time, terms like "web app," "web development," and "custom web programming" don't mean much. If anything, they sound like jargon for those of us who work with websites every day.

That's half-true. But if you're a business owner or executive, there are things you need to know about web programming – not so much *how it's done*, but focused more on *what it can do*. That's what this short book is all about. In the coming pages, I'm going to guide you through the basics of custom web development, including what a web app actually is and how you can have one developed for your business.

Along the way, I'm going to give you some insight into why web programming is so powerful and how you can leverage it to save money, automate tedious tasks, and reach more customers, volunteers, or subscribers than ever before. I'm going to show you how simple pieces of web software, when they are well thought out and designed, can literally transform parts of your business into something more efficient and powerful. The end result is that the more you can automate without sacrificing those needed personal touch areas, the more optimized your business can be for success and efficiency. That's the magic of web programming with business intent.

This isn't a book about the technical process of developing an app, so I'm going to (mostly) skip over the things that actual programmers and developers need to know. Instead, I'm going to focus on the key concepts business people have to be aware of, and what it takes to find the right programming team to work on your behalf. My goal isn't to make you into someone who is going to develop web apps on your own, but to arm you with the information you need to envision a successful web app, choose the right vendor, and then see the project through with a minimum of time, expense, and headaches.

A lot of non-technical business people are scared by terms like "custom web programming." If you're one of them, don't let your anxiety get the best of you. Web coding looks complicated from the outside, but it's really no different than speaking a foreign language or knowing how to use a piece of software like Photoshop or Excel. And as a business person, you don't *have* to know all the details. Having a base of knowledge will make it easier for you to work with your programming team, but you won't have to master any advanced concepts.

With that out of the way, it's time for us to dig in and find out what a web app actually is and how custom web programming can fit into your business model. We'll start at the beginning and take things step by step. By the time we reach the final chapter, you'll be ready to get more than you imagined from your website.

1 | What Is a Web App… and Why Do I Need One?

What is a Web App?

There are a lot of different ways to answer this question. I could begin by telling you that "web app" is short for "website application." Or I could get a little more specific and tell you that a web app is a piece of software that runs on a website, usually right within the browser (like Internet Explorer, Firefox, Safari, Chrome, etc.) you are using at the moment. I could even get into the different things web apps actually do, which we'll talk about later in this book.

If I met you at a cocktail party, however, I wouldn't answer in any of these ways. What I would tell you is simply that a web app is something that can enhance a website, whether it is one section or page within a website or even the entire website itself, to do something it couldn't do before. I would tell you that you use dozens of web apps every week, and probably never knew it, or thought about it, until you needed one or someone pointed it out to you.

The point I'm trying to make is that web apps are ubiquitous. They are everywhere on the Internet, on all the major websites you frequent, and doing lots of little things that people tend to not pay conscious attention to, but that make an enormous difference for the organizations that develop them… not to mention the people that are using them.

So if you're intimidated by the term "web app development," or think that it only applies to tech-minded people, put those thoughts out of your mind. Web apps are business tools, just like the websites they are integrated within. You don't need to know anything about programming to take advantage of them, and deciding to work with a custom web development team doesn't have to make your life or business more complicated. In fact, it's probably going to make a lot of tasks simpler, faster, and less expensive.

That's really what this short book is all about. I'm not going to teach you how to program web apps; instead, I'm first going to show you how you can use them to save time and money day after day, and then provide some high-level insight into the process they go through during creation.

In today's world, having a bit of background knowledge about web apps gives you an advantage over other business owners, executives, and even entire organizations. Once you understand how to make your own operations more efficient with pieces of code, you can spend less on things like labor, inventory, and marketing. Or you can use the gains you receive to spend less time paying attention to details and devote more of your energy to strategic thinking.

You can even use the power of web programming to launch an entirely new enterprise. If you are an entrepreneur with a brand-new web app idea, then having this additional background knowledge can be the spark that brings your new business to life.

With those initial concepts out of the way, let's take a closer look at what a web app actually is.

The Anatomy of a Web App

I've already explained that a web app is basically just a piece of software that runs within a web browser. But even though that rough description gives you a sense of what a web app *is*, it doesn't really help business people put a finger on how they are actually used, or what they really represent.

In order to get a little bit deeper, let's begin by mentioning a couple of things that web apps *aren't*. First, you should know that web apps are different from the native smartphone and tablet apps you probably use every day. Although the two are related, and both are sometimes referred to as simply "apps," they tend to serve different purposes.

Native phone and tablet apps are usually downloaded as standalone pieces of software. They perform simple tasks, like helping you to log on to a specialized version of a website or to organize your shopping list, and function in a way that is completely independent from other apps and websites. To put this another way, you can run the Google app on your iPhone without having to open up Google in a web browser at the same time.

The web applications we are thinking about work in a similar way, but run in the background of an actual website that the visitor is interacting with. They aren't typically bought or downloaded by the end user, which makes them more accessible to customers, prospects, and employees. Instead, they function behind the scenes, making it easier to accomplish or automate certain tasks *all within a web browser.*

Because confusion can exist about these two similar types of software, you may notice that I will stick with the terms "web app" and "web application" throughout this book. That isn't because I enjoy repetition, but because shortening things to "app" can cause confusion. Just remember that we're talking about programs small or large that run in the background of a website, not anything you download to a tablet or mobile device.

With the distinction between mobile apps and web apps out of the way, let's take a look at the difference between a *web app* and a *website.* This is an area where the lines and differences tend to get a little bit blurrier.

If you were to follow the strict definitions of each, you could easily make the case that all websites are web applications. After all, they allow users to access them and conduct actions, even if those actions are just reading text and viewing images. If you were to spend some time in online forums for programmers and developers (and wanted to waste hours of your life), you would actually find variations of this debate.

That's fine, and the arguments are valid. Really though, these kinds of discussions come down to semantics, and that's not what we're shooting for in this book. With that in mind, I'm going to stick to the traditional definitions and differences: A web design is generally thought of as layouts, text, and images, while web development (and the resulting web applications) has to do with those underlying bits of software that perform certain tasks.

Regardless of what you call them, or how you draw the line between one and another, it's clear that web design and web development should always go hand-in-hand. You can't do much with great custom programming if you're placing your web apps on a terrible website. Likewise – and this is something that a lot of business owners *and* web designers forget – a website that looks great but doesn't incorporate any sort of programming is little better than an online brochure. Both elements are strictly important.

This concept is incredibly easy to illustrate once we start looking at a few common web apps and how they function within a website. For example, nearly 100% of everyone reading this book will have used an online shopping cart at some point. That's an example of a relatively simple piece of web programming. Without that unique bit of code, running in the background beyond your immediate attention, a website wouldn't be able to work with your browser to "remember" which items you want to buy and what price they are supposed to be, calculate shipping, and so on.

Another everyday example of web programming would be content that changes based on where you're from or what you've previously viewed. By working with cookies and other small bits of tracking code, websites can display headlines, ads, and even entirely customized pages based on your history. A simple website with a set of pages that can be visited can't accomplish this job, but with a bit of custom programming, you can give every visitor a unique (or at least a targeted) experience.

As a final example, consider the chat boxes that are now popular as a way to enhance sales and customer service. Again, these run in the background of a website, and visitors don't give them much thought. But with a proper program in place, visitors can get in touch with someone who can help them instantly and in real time. That little piece of software helps make communication more convenient, and saves time on both ends of the business relationship.

When you consider those three simple examples of web applications and the way they work, it's easy to see why design and development have to go together. You simply can't get the most of one without the other.

For the sake of discussion throughout the rest of this book, consider web design to be about looks and content, and web development as being concerned with functionality and features. As I said, the lines can be a bit blurry, but that shouldn't be your concern as a business person. You can let the programmers argue about what they want to call their work, so long as you get the resulting website you need... and one that does everything you and your customers want it to.

Why Do You Need Web Development?

Having shed just a little bit of light on what a web app actually is, let's get back to the real question that should be on your mind: *Why do you need web apps?* And, even closer to the point, *why should you bother reading the rest of this book to learn more about the web app development process?*

The answer, in both cases, is incredibly simple – web apps help your business do more. They aren't just bits of software – they are shortcuts that let you manage people, products, services and interactions in a smarter, more efficient way.

You need web apps because you have a website but want to generate more sales. You have them developed because you're sick of seeing opportunities go to waste when customers aren't added to the right marketing lists. You invested a few hours and learned about them because you want to give yourself, and your organization, a massive edge over everyone else who doesn't know or understand very much about web development.

Web design is about the way your online presence looks, but web development is about what it can actually do. That's the difference between spending money on a website and earning a positive return on your investment for months and years to come.

I can't emphasize enough that web apps aren't just bits of software, but tools for bottom-line business growth. In the same way that an automated telephone system is less about routing phone calls than it is about smarter customer service, web application development is more a function of creating smarter processes than it is adding new software to your servers.

Throughout the coming chapters we'll look in greater depth at web apps, their uses, and the process of brainstorming and developing them from a business person's point of view. For the moment, though, you've gained an understanding of what a web app is, how it can be used, and why smart companies invest in them. That puts you miles ahead of most of your colleagues, and it's a great place for us to start on this quick learning journey.

Who Am I to Teach You About Web Apps?

Before you take my word for anything, you might want to know who I am and why I've written this book. Because I know your time is as valuable as mine, I'll stick to the highlights.

My name is Paul J. Scott, and I've been in the web development and design industry for the better part of two decades. Several years ago, I left my corporate job and began my own firm, GoingClear Interactive (based right in Boston, Massachusetts), that specializes in web design and development for businesses large and small, nonprofits, government agencies, and educational institutions of all sizes.

In some ways, I feel like I've *always* been in web development... even going back to the days before I had my first computer. As a second grader, I remember "contracting" for my two sisters – at the exorbitant rate of five dollars per session – to help them come up with a plan to clean and optimize their bedrooms. I would draw a written diagram, think of the ways they needed to access different parts of their rooms, and then start to move furniture and objects around in my mind. Pretty soon, I would be able to envision just where everything would go. That satisfaction was even better than earning my tiny fee.

That early process of listening and planning served me well during my teen years, where I grew up caddying for business leaders on Nantucket's Sankaty Head golf course. I learned even more about strategizing, both on the links and throughout life in general.

Since those humble beginnings, I have worked on hundreds of web development projects, from simple shopping cart installations to large, data-base-driven websites with thousands of dynamic pages and secure areas. I've seen the good, the bad, and the ugly, but most importantly I've seen how custom web programming can revitalize a business, or even build one from scratch.

I've also seen what kinds of mistakes clients and their programming teams can make, as well as the pitfalls that stand in the way of your success as a business owner, executive, or entrepreneur.

Throughout all of this, my biggest frustration in my professional life has been watching others struggle with the concept of web development, or ultimately choose to go without it because they either didn't recognize the opportunities in front of them or thought they'd have to master lots of technical details to take advantage of them.

By writing this book, I'm doing my part to educate business leaders about simple tools and techniques they can use to automate processes, increase efficiency, and save time and money on a permanent basis. By reading it, you're ensuring that you won't be one of those people who watches bottom-line improvement float by simply because you haven't heard about a few core concepts, or don't pursue your passion because you're intimidated by the web development process.

If that sounds good to you, let's get to work on learning how businesses use custom web programming to increase their profitability...

2 | How Businesses Use Web Programming Profitably

Because web apps are so versatile, there are hundreds (or maybe even thousands) of ways you could use them to make your website more versatile and powerful. Because custom web programming can make processes faster, safer, and more reliable, they have a variety of uses.

The truth of custom programming is that you are limited only by your imagination and the talent of the team you're working with. Below, you'll find some of the more common ways companies put custom web applications to use. How many of them could you integrate into your own website and business plan?

Automation

This is arguably the biggest and most common use for web programming. There are literally thousands of processes that can be automated using simple web apps, making life easier for end users *and* the organizations that develop them.

For an easy example, suppose you want to schedule a visit with a medical specialist. Instead of showing up early in their waiting room and filling out dozens of forms, one after another, the receptionist scheduling your appointment could take your email address and send you a link. Upon clicking that link, you'd be taken to an online version of the form with your relevant contact information, medical history, current complaints, and so on.

By giving you the chance to complete your paperwork in advance, the medical practice is making it easier and less stressful for you to get the care you need. At the same time, they are saving on staff hours, reducing the odds that an error will be introduced into your records, and likely decreasing the amount of time you have to spend waiting for your doctor to see you.

This is a simple but common example of the way automation works. It's a powerful concept, and one with many uses. Best of all, web apps for automation tend to be simple and inexpensive, so there's no good reason for businesses not to put them to use.

Marketing

As with automation, the uses for web apps as a means of increasing marketing range and efficiency are essentially endless. The web is awash with information and analytics. Web apps can be used to collect more of that information, analyze it more effectively, and use it in a more precise way.

To get a sense of why this is, consider that a person who visits your website and interacts with your content gives you several pieces of information even if they never fill out a single form. First, their IP gives you some idea of the region they are coming from, and possibly the language (or languages) they speak. If you have a good website analytics package installed, you may even know what they searched to find your website in the first place.

Once they start using your website, they tell you, in essence, about the things that interest them through the links they follow and the amount of time they spend on each page.

With the right web app in place, you could gather more information from or about your visitors. Or, even more powerfully, you could change the way offers are displayed to them based on demographics, viewing patterns, and other criteria that change and present themselves *in real time*.

In other words, your website could respond and adapt itself to individual visitors, or follow up with them in ways that acknowledge prior interactions. Handled correctly, the goal can only be increased conversions and higher profits – something you wouldn't get from a static website, but that is infinitely possible with custom web development.

E-commerce

E-commerce and web development have grown up side by side, and for good reason: Growth in one area spurs growth in another. Shopping carts and integrated payment solutions were among the first forms of web apps to be widely used, and since then online stores of all sizes have utilized custom programming to help meet bottom-line goals.

Small pieces of software can be used to improve e-commerce by automating the ordering and re-ordering process, offering advanced (and personalized) marketing features to individual buyers, creating add-on sales during the check-out process, and updating inventory and shipping information in real time, to name just a few.

Whether you want to sell more products, accept and publish online reviews, or just streamline the flow of orders through your fulfillment system, a web app developed specifically for your online store – or a customization to your existing e-commerce framework – can be the key to bigger sales and a higher profit margin.

Customer Service

Using custom web development, companies can greatly reduce customer service expenditures while actually offering a better standard of care to buyers. That's because they can monitor interactions, set responses, and even offer customer retention specials all based on predefined criteria.

Combining customer service with automation is a powerful way to take advantage of web development. Think of the example I gave before, of patients submitting information to a medical provider. Now, envision the many dozens of ways businesses interact with their customers again and again – updating contact information, replacing orders, changing subscriptions, etc. – and then think of how much more efficiently these tasks can be handled by a simple piece of web-based software.

That doesn't just apply to external customers, either. The internal routing of information from one department to the next, or even one database to another, can be handled by a piece of web-based software that won't require a salary, make transcription mistakes, or stop working past business hours.

Adding just a small amount of functionality to your website can help you keep more of your customers year after year, and encourage them to place larger orders with your company.

Feeds

The interactive nature of the World Wide Web means that we are always sending and receiving information from a lot of different sources. In the social age, having feed-driven web apps can be a way to connect with visitors in a whole new way.

You've probably already experienced this, at least in a basic sense, when you last visited one of your favorite websites and saw a handful of the company's latest tweets or Facebook updates. While social feeding is an ongoing trend, web apps can draw information from a variety of sources and display them online – even in a way that is specific to a particular visitor.

Things like stock prices, sports scores, job openings, and shipping status can all be updated via automated or specialized feeds. These feeds make your website more useful to visitors and more engaging to the people you do business with, all while requiring very little in the way of custom web programming after the initial setup.

Database Interaction

Lists and databases are at the heart of operations for every organization that has more than a few buyers or employees. The bigger and more complex the organization gets, the more lists – in the form of databases – there are to be managed, segmented, and updated.

As you might imagine, this is the kind of task that web apps excel at. With just a few keystrokes, someone who's interested in your product or service can give you their contact information. With the right piece of custom web software in place, you can automatically add them to the right lists, update their subscription info, and make sure you use your new lead to its best possible purpose.

That's just one example, of course. Custom web programming can be used to manage customers, subscriptions, employees, volunteers, donors, addresses, and even thousands of products or inventory items. No matter how many parts of your business are database-driven (and there are usually a lot more than you would think of, off the top of your head), there's probably a web programming solution that could help things run more smoothly.

Security

Online security is a big topic within custom web programming, if only because you don't want to leave vulnerabilities on your website that could come back to haunt you later. That's a topic we will explore in a later section. For the moment, though, note that web apps can also be used to bolster your existing level of security in many ways.

One simple use would be a web app that pays close attention to certain types of risk factors and repels attacks from malicious visitors. Another good idea is to use web apps to restrict access to intra-webs or members-only sections of your online content. You could even use custom web programming to bar certain types of visits or interactions altogether.

Security is one of those topics that is typically very unique to an individual situation, so I won't go into much greater length here. However, never forget that while it's important to consider web security in the context of making sure your web app doesn't leave "open doors" on your website, you can use them to tighten up existing security, as well.

A Unique Experience

While I've been giving you some examples of the way web apps have been used effectively and profitably in the past, it's important to note that the best way to integrate custom web programming into your website may be through something completely new that I (or anyone else) haven't even thought of yet.

As we'll see in the next chapter, some of the best web programming is actually creative in nature, especially when it comes to brainstorming new web applications and how they integrate into visitor experience. If there is something you'd like to see handled more smoothly, quickly, or automatically, it is probably a good target for custom programming.

So, as you consider this list, remember that it covers many of the important bases but is by no means comprehensive. At their heart, Google, Airbnb, and Uber are all just web apps. One began with the simple idea that a better formula could help web searchers find what they're looking for faster; the other two grew from the inspiration that things like cars and homes could help their owners make a little more money than they normally would sitting idle.

Every great web app starts with a concept, even if that concept doesn't fit neatly into one of the boxes I've already described. If you can dream it, a good custom web development team can probably build it... and it can help your company grow, if not explode with massive growth.

Two Important Benefits of Custom Web-Based Programming

Now that you're thinking about some of the ways web apps could be used to improve your company and streamline processes in marketing, customer service, and other areas, it's time to address two quick questions. The first is why you should use a web app instead of an offline application, especially when both might be available to accomplish the same thing. The second is whether you should consider custom web programming or a readily available application for the same job, if one exists.

In the first case, web apps have a couple of big advantages over offline software. The most obvious is that they can be altered, updated, and re-implemented almost in an instant. The second you change your web app and upload the new version, it is immediately available for everyone to use and benefit from. That wouldn't be the case with a piece of software that resides on a physical machine and needed to be updated via disk or download.

Also, web apps can actually be safer than offline software, despite the belief a lot of business people hold to the contrary. Because static pieces of software can be studied and broken, with the weaknesses shared among many people, it only takes a single crack for someone to alter or steal the code you've paid to produce. Attacks on a web app, on the other hand, can be discovered quickly and security can be put into place.

So what about the second question of whether you should opt for custom web development or license an existing piece of software?

There isn't a good set answer. Much depends on the quality of the software available, and the price, as well as the issue of how well it matches up to the job you need it to perform. In some cases, you can purchase a web app, add it to your site, and have it perform flawlessly. In fact, there are numerous apps available for things like e-commerce and social feeding that are nearly ready to use "off the shelf."

The downside to using available web apps is that they might not do exactly what you want them to do, and altering them can sometimes violate the licensing agreements you signed when you purchased them. Additionally, there are some instances in which you might not want to be using the same kinds of apps as your colleagues and competitors, either because they aren't tailored to your specific business or don't give you any strategic advantage.

Another thing to consider with popular web apps is that the more people you have using a specific piece of software, the more incentive there is for a criminal to try to crack it. So even though most web apps are very safe, you'll want to be careful about what you add to your website.

The best answer is usually to envision the things you need your website to do (following the process we'll lay out in the next chapter), and then work with a team of programmers you can trust to decide whether the app should be built from scratch, altered from a pre-existing piece of software, or purchased and uploaded.

3 | Finding a Great Web App Concept

What do you want your web app to do? How do you want it to change your business? Or what business do you want to build based on your new web app concept? There are probably a thousand or more great answers to these questions. In the last chapter, we explored some of the more common uses for web development, but this book isn't about understanding how other organizations take advantage of programming – it's about figuring out what your company can do to increase sales, save money, and make processes simpler.

It's worth mentioning again that, although most business people tend to think of things like software development as being a purely technical exercise, the reality is that it's often creative work first and foremost. That's especially true when it comes to generating concepts for web apps.

You might be able to take a largely "hands-off" approach to the rest of the web development process, but when it comes to envisioning the things that the software on your website can actually do, and help with, you should be guiding progress at every step. It's likely the team you choose to design your website and develop your web apps will have some input and suggestions, but they don't know your business, your customers, and your objectives the way you do. They can't tell you what you actually need, but they can listen and assist in developing a fine-tuned web app that meets your requirements and then some.

To that end, you could probably come up with a great set of web app concepts just by brainstorming different ideas to make your organization more efficient. While you could begin with a blank slate, it's probably easier to get started if you have a bit of inspiration to nudge you in the right direction. We've learned over the years that, sometimes, inspiration can be born out of frustration with inefficiencies.

Let's look at a handful of simple ways you can discover web app concepts that help you to develop something special for your business...

Ask Customers and Employees

If you want to know what your most important customers and employees need, why not simply ask them? While you might not want to frame your inquiries in terms of web development (which your staff and customers might not fully understand), just figuring out what they wish they could get from your website can be a positive step in the right direction.

The beauty of this approach is that it can yield simple, powerful answers that you might not have come up with on your own. Sometimes, we can be too close to the challenges of our own business to fully understand what buyers really want from us, for example, or the realities that front-line employees face. In some instances, they can make suggestions for small, inexpensive changes and improvements that can reduce frustration, streamline everyday operations, and help you hold on to more customers.

Of course, not every suggestion you receive is likely to be useful and actionable. But by soliciting feedback from lots of different customers, and several layers of your organization, you should be able to get useful feedback that can help drive your web app development project forward.

Find Bottlenecks in Your Business

As you already probably understand by this point in the book, web apps are great for clearing problem areas and inefficiencies out of everyday work. So if you regularly have bottlenecks in your business that prevent things from moving forward as quickly as you'd like, developing a web app to "smooth out the edges" can be a great idea.

A good example of this can often be found in data entry. Most organizations, no matter how big or small, end up spending significant amounts of time and money entering things like customer addresses, product codes, and other details into various mailing lists or CRM systems. These jobs are tedious but necessary. Outsourcing is an option, but can lead to costly errors being made repeatedly by vendors who are either working quickly to turn a profit or simply don't understand what the data represents.

Handling these tasks with custom web programming is a less expensive and more reliable alternative, and one that gives you a permanent fix to an ongoing issue. Wherever there are bottlenecks in your business – especially those related to logistics, data, or paperwork – web app development can be the perfect solution.

Locate Unnecessary Expenses

Another great way to generate ideas for your web app is simply by studying your bottom line and looking for expense items that come up again and again. Even if the expenses in question can't be eliminated altogether, there might be room for improvement with a little bit of programming and/or automation.

Suppose, for example, that one of your biggest line items each quarter is shipping. Having a web app that integrates inventory, multiple distribution centers, and shipping provider details might easily help you to save a few percentage points on that cost category month after month. Over time, those savings could add up to something substantial. That's money you could put back into other areas of your business, or hold on to as additional profit.

In some other cases, you might be able to eliminate extra expenses altogether. For example, with a little bit of custom programming to integrate your CRM with an online database, you could give customers a "paperless billing" option that would eliminate the need for printing, postage meter expenses, and other costs permanently.

The possibilities here go on and on. Looking through your balance sheet and profit and loss statements is a great way to find inspiration for web development, or at least will get your mind moving in the right direction.

Look for New Sales Opportunities

I have already made the point that web app development can help grow sales, but it's an idea you should take to heart, especially if your website has e-commerce features (or you plan to add them in the future).

Simple web apps can enhance your shopping cart, suggest products to customers based on their self-identified preferences or shopping habits, and help you to "upsell" things like accessories and warranty items. In each case, you aren't just improving the odds of making a bigger sale, but you're also paving the way for *future* sales by adding convenience in your online store.

Offline, there are ways you can use custom web programming to increase sales too, especially through the use of automated CRM updates and list segmentation. The more you know your prospects – and the more you know about what they want and need – the more of them you're going to be able to convert into customers... and the easier time you'll have holding on to those customers later.

With a bit of careful thinking, you can probably come up with several different ways to use web programming to increase sales, both at the point of purchase and through long-term customer retention.

Imagine a Better User Experience

What might your customers wish they could do with your website or company, but isn't currently being offered? This is a broad question, but also a very important one.

To see why, let's go back to an example we gave earlier in the book of automation and customer service. Perhaps buyers wish they could log in to their accounts, change their contact and billing details, or have the flexibility to repeat previous orders with the click of a mouse. Earlier, we focused on how adding these features can help reduce your costs. It's worth pointing out again, though, that they also make things more convenient for the men and women who do business with you and might not have the time to pick up the phone during the day.

Integrating features like a search bar for content, an online chat session for technical support, interactive versions of product manuals, and real-time shipping updates all give customers a better experience working with your business. That makes them more satisfied and keeps them coming back, which helps your business performance in the long run.

By imagining what customers want (or finding out by asking them), you can develop web app concepts that can change your organization in the blink of an eye.

Integrate Online and Offline Tools

If your business relies on a custom piece of software that's already been built, or specialized tools that are standard in your industry, a bit of web programming might be all that's needed to expand its features or add them to your website.

There are numerous possibilities in this area, many of them coming back to the ongoing theme of automation. Tasks like billing, scheduling, and inventory management are often handled by pieces of software that are expensive and particular to a certain type of company. If they aren't integrated with your website, you're probably losing out on the added efficiency you would get from transferring information from one platform to another.

Because the solution you need to help you integrate online and offline tools depends largely on which tools you're using, we won't go into greater depth on this point. Just know that it's worth talking to your web development team about the ways you can make the parts of your business work together more smoothly, even if they didn't develop the software or application you need to coordinate with.

Borrow Inspiration from Others

They say imitation is the highest form of flattery. Whether you believe that or not, it's certainly true that a lot of organizations get the inspiration for their web apps from other concepts or processes they've seen in use. More often than not, the web app they've noticed doesn't even come from the same industry; just as a painting can inspire a novel, a web app developed for manufacturing can spur on new innovations in e-commerce and vice versa.

As you consider the various ways you could put custom web development to use on your website, don't be afraid to have a look around some of your favorite websites and see what kinds of tools and functionality they are using. Are there elements you could add to your own website that would make it more powerful, useful, or profitable?

Find Ways to Redefine Your Business

Some of the very best web development is done on behalf of entrepreneurs who want to bring something new to their business or industry. They come to a programming team with an idea to revolutionize the way things work, or have a vague vision of how business might be done, and then use that inspiration to change the game for everyone.

I mention this here for two reasons. The first is to remind you that entrepreneurs and startups have a certain advantage with web app development; they might not have big budgets to work with, but they do tend to have open minds. Creativity is king when it comes to generating and nurturing web app concepts. The second reason is to remind you to think big. While there's nothing wrong with using web apps to automate and refine simple processes, don't limit yourself to minor everyday applications – don't be afraid to come up with something fantastic that could turn your website into the gold standard for your industry.

Technology can be used to refine just about any part of your business, and web apps bring automation and interactivity to every department or process. Ask yourself "what if?" and then let the answer take you to a profitable web app that your prospects, customers or employees will love.

Merging Concepts with Capabilities

One thing you certainly *shouldn't* do while brainstorming web app concepts, at least in the beginning, is worry about whether or not your ideas are feasible. I encourage you to take an "anything is possible" approach to the task, imagining that you'll be able to get everything you want from your web programming team.

Pragmatism has its place – but it shouldn't be your primary concern when you're coming up with concepts. Later, when you have a list of concepts to take to your team, you can let them evaluate your concepts and tell you which ones will be easier or more difficult to implement.

In most web development projects, it's not a matter of figuring out *whether* your idea can be developed or not, but whether it makes sense from a business perspective. In other words, will your finished web app be worth the cost of the development project to see the final project through? Will it makes sense to pursue the concept once you've seen a budget, considered the alternatives, and thought about other tools users can take advantage of… or other web apps you could develop?

For simple and straightforward tasks, like those involving automation and information sharing (feeds) from one platform to another, costs are usually minimal. For more complex operations and integrations, more wireframing, programming, and testing might be required. We'll address these subjects in the coming chapters, but the key point here is that your web app concept can always be simplified, altered, or even put off until later if the numbers don't work out. Later, we'll look at some ways you can cut the initial development costs down by envisioning a scaled-back version of your web app to start with. None of those considerations matter, though, if you don't brainstorm the idea for the web app in the first place.

Generate as many different concepts as you can, working on your own, with your staff, and even with outside customers or vendors. Give yourself the luxury of having many, many choices to work with and then prioritize them later. There will be a time to bring some ideas down to earth when considering schedules, budgets, and capabilities. Just don't miss out on a million-dollar idea because you assume it can't work. You might be surprised!

4 | Web App Development For Startups

In a lot of ways, web development is similar from one project, website, or company to the next. Regardless of the specific challenge or organization, the process of programming a new page or piece of web software (something we'll cover soon) is more or less the same.

There is an exception to that rule, though: Designing websites and web apps for startups is an endeavor that's unique enough to deserve its own chapter. That's because startups have different needs and limitations than other businesses, and some opportunities, too.

Although startups can and do use web apps in the same ways that other companies do, entrepreneurs are sometimes best positioned to take advantage of custom web programming. This is partly because they often don't have websites or established processes in place to begin with. That is, they are working with a "blank slate" and can take advantage of any good idea that saves time and money without having to worry about how it will affect existing software customer interactions.

In some situations, the development of a new web app or concept might be core to the differentiating principle of the business itself. In other words, entrepreneurs may be able to brainstorm and integrate web apps that their competitors haven't even thought of, and wouldn't be able to take advantage of. This can give them a semi-permanent advantage, or at least a big jumpstart in the marketplace.

The flipside to this, of course, is that startups need to be careful about the web development processes they follow. They need to be extra careful to choose the right partners, test their web apps, and think their concepts through from beginning to end. That's because a single bad user experience – or worse, an issue with stability or security – can be fatal to a company that's relying on its website, which is built around their web app, for revenue growth.

Still, even though a word of caution is warranted, these fears shouldn't deter entrepreneurs from pursuing web development aggressively in the first place. Entire businesses (eBay, Uber, and Amazon come to mind) have essentially been built on a simple concept backed by the strength of some innovative web programming. Pioneers in e-commerce have left their competitors behind because they were better able to automate the process of ordering, inventory, shipping, and delivery; other businesses have streamlined the customer experience to the point where buyers *hate* to do their shopping elsewhere.

Behind every entrepreneurial vision is a new way of doing things, and that's the same driving force that leads to great web app development. If you have a startup, or are contemplating one, now is the perfect time to envision the ways you could leapfrog others in your industry or category with custom web programming.

Get Creative

The one thing you simply cannot imitate, duplicate, or replace in web app development – or anywhere else in the Internet – is creative thinking. The digital world thrives on the ideas that people just like you generate, and you never know which one could be the winner that opens new doors you would never have imagined.

Countless startups have been launched by people with no business or Internet experience – they simply "had a good idea" and decided to run with it. Who knows how many countless others *could* have succeeded if only someone with a bit of inspiration would have followed through to see where it might lead?

The point I'm trying to make here is that I want you to think creatively and to pay attention to that little voice in your head that tells you that you have stumbled onto a good idea when you hear it. Don't doubt or dismiss yourself just because you don't know much about creating a website, because you're sure someone must've thought of it already, or because your last idea didn't work.

You don't need to be a successful billionaire to have a great idea for a website, and you don't have to launch a billion-dollar business to be successful with web development. All it takes is an idea for a website or tool that *could* exist, and be helpful, along with a willingness to do a bit of research and planning.

It's been said that every single person on earth has a million-dollar idea at least once in their lifetimes, but few of us ever decide to pursue the shreds of inspiration that come our way. No matter who you are, where you live, or how you work, you have ideas and insights that no one else does. Why not put them to use by thinking creatively about a new website app development project?

Look at the Competition, But Don't Obsess About Them

At least once a month, I hear from someone who has had a wonderful idea for a web app, only to discover that another business has already launched a similar service. What follows is usually a thought process that goes something like: "Oh well, I guess it's back to the drawing board..."

My default response to that kind of notion is *not so fast*. While there are some parts of the online market that are so effectively competitive as to be closed off, they are few and far between.

The easiest way to explain this is just by driving down the street. If you're like most of us, you probably have several high-profile fast food chains in your neighborhood. Even though one or two of them dominate the market, spending hundreds of millions on advertising, new competitors successfully enter the industry all the time. In many cases, buyers are glad to see them, because they bring additional choices to the market.

So while you might not want to take on Kayak and Expedia directly with your own all-in-one travel website, know that there might be plenty of room for your regional web app that allows users to see reviews and make reservations. That's just an example, of course, but the point here is that you should look for competition, and examine it, but not obsess about it. Just because someone else is making money in a certain business or category doesn't mean that you can't too.

In fact, I go as far as to say that a lack of competition can actually be a bad thing. When you have an idea for a new web app, and can't find anything similar that's already available, that should tell you one of two things: either your idea is truly innovative, or others have tried to do something similar and weren't able to turn a profit from it.

When you see a few different companies in the business you're trying to break into, you at least know that there are some successful business models in place. That's a good starting point for any entrepreneurial endeavor, so learn to see other businesses as a source of information, and not just a group of competitors who want to crowd you out.

Scrutinize Your Revenue Model Closely

Occasionally, I meet with men and women who have a wonderful idea for a web app development project, except for one little detail… they can't figure out how they'll make any money from it.

This is more common than you might think, and would-be entrepreneurs are sometimes tempted to ignore their business instincts and push through toward an idea that they love. That's understandable, but it's also a good way to blow through a small fortune without getting much in return.

Don't get me wrong – building a successful web app is satisfying in its own right, and money isn't the best (or only) goal for launching a new website. However, if you ignore the financial side of things for too long, it's very likely that your web development project either won't get finished or won't grow into the kind of platform you hoped it would become. Launching a new website with custom features takes a bit of capital, and those bills have to be paid somehow.

Luckily, developing a successful revenue model is often a simple matter of brainstorming. There are a lot of different ways that a website can make money for you. Here are a few of the most common:

Advertising revenue – If you build a great web app, and one that's useful to a certain kind of person, then it's only a matter of time before the companies who sell to those people will come knocking and see if they can get a piece of the pie. Depending on the popularity of your website, and the industry it promotes, the advertising revenue you earn from a successful web app can range from steady to substantial.

Referral fees – Although this is really just another form of advertising revenue, it deserves mention in its own category. Let's say you develop a website that provides specific advice and information on cosmetic dental care. It's a good bet that dentists around the country who specialize in cosmetic dental work would be willing to pay a good fee for each qualified referral you send their way. Generally speaking, the difference between "advertising" and "referrals" is specificity within a geographic region or a type of business.

Subscriptions – If you would prefer to go without advertisers, or want to add additional revenue streams to your website, you can charge users directly to take advantage of the service or information you're offering. As with referral fees, this type of monetization usually works best when you have targeted specific industry, and a type of buyer who is very concerned or committed to a certain topic.

Direct product or service sales – This is arguably the most common and successful way to earn revenue from your web development project. Whether e-commerce is the main focus of your website or just an additional way to process sales, giving visitors the option to buy things directly from your website is a good way to improve your bottom-line picture.

Whichever revenue model (or combination of models) you prefer, it's a good idea to decide which ones you want to pursue early on in your web development project. This is important on one level because it helps you to aim your efforts, and your brainstorming, toward a more tangible end goal that's easy to visualize. It also influences the way app interfaces will be modeled, since you'll want users to have easy interactions that steer them toward revenue-producing activities.

In a different way, this is important because it will let you start thinking through the financial implications of your web development project. It's unfortunate, but a lot of creative teams will be happy to take your money, and build a web app for you, even if they don't think you'll ever see a positive return from your investment.

With an experienced programming team, like the one I have at GoingClear Interactive, the issue is hardly ever "Can we build this?" but instead "Should we build this?" In other words, we almost always have the capabilities, but we want to be sure that our clients have realistic, sustainable business plans to go forward with once our work is done.

A good web development team is going to help you work through these possibilities, but you should scrutinize your revenue model prior to meeting with potential vendors.

Anticipate Major Roadblocks

Even if you have a great web app concept and a proven revenue model, there are still roadblocks that can kill your project in its tracks... or doom it from the start. Typically, these fall into one of two categories: legal or logistical.

For an easy-to-understand example of how a great web app can be ruined by the fine print, consider a hypothetical project (but one that's based on the kinds of issues we've seen clients run into). Suppose you want to build a web app that allows users to log in, enter the serial numbers for various products, and see what kinds of warranties and/or returns are available to them in real time. It might even show them where to turn if they have a service issue, and help them to print necessary forms and log warranty claims.

Such a service would be very helpful to a lot of people, and would save them time digging through old receipts and manuals. And yet, it wouldn't be all that likely to ever see the light of day.

The reason is simple: Putting together this kind of web app would require integration with lots of different manufacturers and retailers, many of which would not be likely to cooperate. And on the other end, customers would have to submit detailed information – including serial numbers – about their possessions. While some people might be willing to do that, concerns over theft, targeted marketing, etc., would undoubtedly put some users off.

To shift to the legal side of things, let's suppose you want to build a website that lets users trade sports and celebrity memorabilia. There might be an audience, and a profit to be made, but securing things like copyright permissions and image rights could be a major (and expensive) obstacle. There are a lot of different things that can go wrong when others own the content or materials you want to use in your web app.

These are just hypothetical situations, but the fact of the matter is that lots of people come to us with really great web app ideas that have a fatal flaw. It's important that you recognize where the weaknesses of your concept might be and develop plans to overcome them before you get too deep into the development process. Otherwise, you could waste a lot of time and money just to discover that your web app isn't going to be the guaranteed success you hoped it would become.

Find Your MVP

Once you're sure your web app concept is feasible – or have refined it to the point that it has become realistic – it's time to find your MVP, or *minimum viable product.*

The idea behind in MVP is simple: Instead of turning your web app into a huge project with every tool or feature you can imagine crammed in, you create a stripped-down version of the site and/or software that's functional, but without all the bells and whistles. It's a simpler, streamlined version of your web app that can be built in less time, and with a smaller cash outlay.

The MVP is incredibly useful because it allows you to jump into the market with a minimum of money spent. Budgets are almost always a concern for startups, and developing a bare-bones version of your web app – instead of a bigger, more expensive project with every feature you can imagine – is a good way to reduce the size of your initial investment and get revenue coming in more quickly.

Also, developing an MVP allows you to let your ideas grow organically without permanently constraining you to any particular interface or feature list. This is important for any web development project, since web apps tend to grow and evolve as they are programmed and tested — but it's especially crucial to startups who might not have a great deal of market awareness. In other words, you might not know what you want your finished web app to look like until you've already launched an earlier version of it. Putting a minimum viable product online allows you to test the waters and see where you're going next.

There are any number of ways to scale back your web app concept to create an MVP. Perhaps you can begin with just a few products or databases, or start by serving a single area or type of customer. Maybe you won't need as much content to start as you would for a bigger rollout.

A good web development team can help you find the parameters for your MVP and show you how it can grow and expand in the future. For now, keep in mind that your first "finished" version of your web app doesn't have to have everything you're hoping for in the final version. It can be something to start with and build on, saving you a lot of time and money as you learn and refine your business model.

When in Doubt, Don't Be Afraid to Ask

In this chapter, I've given you a lot of different factors to think about, and these are on top of the normal entrepreneurial concerns like funding, cash flow, setting up a legal business structure, and so on.

If it seems like a lot to consider, keep in mind you don't have to do all of this brainstorming alone. Even though you should be aware of the key concepts and considerations that I've mentioned, you don't necessarily have to have all of the answers when you get started. There are experts you can turn to.

In the next chapter, we're going to look at some steps you can take to find a great web development partner to work with. One of the qualities you need, of course, is a consultative approach – a team of experienced web programmers who can explain not only what they'll do for you, but the process they'll follow and the decisions you'll need to make along the way.

Chances are, there are going to be a lot of those decisions... and a lot of questions you'll need answers to before you get started. That's okay. The important thing is that you end up with a good web app concept and have a knowledge of the issues that matter most to startups. From there, the right vendor can help you find your way.

5 | Choosing a Web Development Partner

At some point between your initial inspiration and the launching of your new web app, you're going to have to choose a vendor to help you turn your vision into a reality.

This is a bigger decision than a lot of business people think. As I've already stated, most people outside the web design and development industry tend to think of programming as something technical. As long as you know what you need, the thinking goes, you can find the cheapest provider, or even an overseas company, to build it for you.

Television shows and movies perpetuate this idea, with "coders" and "hackers" working – unbathed and unshaven – in dark rooms for days on end, pouring over nonsensical strings of language that magically turn into custom software. While there are certainly some programmers who fit that mold, and it's true that programming looks like gibberish if you don't understand it, the reality is that it's closer to writing than it is doing algebra.

In other words, programming custom web apps has a creative element, in addition to the technical details that have to be mastered. That's important, because if you choose a firm that has the right qualifications, but no experience or creativity, you'll be limiting the potential of your web app at best, and very dissatisfied with the results.

In this chapter, I'm going to give you a bird's-eye view of what you need to look for in a web development partner. Let's start with the basics...

Look for Experience and Expertise

When you start looking at different web development companies, you'll quickly find that many of them are all too happy to show you what their technical qualifications are like. They work with dozens of languages and platforms, and probably have lots of degrees and certifications.

These are all wonderful qualifications, and they make a good starting point. But seeing a programming group's technical qualifications is like reviewing the GPA on someone's résumé – it's an interesting detail to consider, but it only tells you so much about the candidate.

To really get great work, you want a team with high-level expertise *and* experience working with lots of different kinds of websites and web apps. You'll certainly want to know that they've worked with applications like the one you're considering, of course, but also that they've been able to take on a whole spectrum of other large and small projects, as well.

Why should you care whether your web development team has a diverse portfolio of past clients and projects? That's easy – because of that creative element I already mentioned. The bigger and more complex your web app will be (or could become in the future), the more types of skill and experience are going to be needed to add features, make it stable, and keep things secure.

There is no teacher like experience, and that's certainly true in web development, where even simple errors in coding can cause big problems that linger, cause a poor user experience, or delay the release of your web app for weeks on end. Finding a development team with lots of certifications on the wall is good... but being able to work with one who can understand how the different pieces of custom web software work together is even better.

Check Out Case Studies and Previous Work

Once you have a sense of the development team's general experience level and capabilities, it's time to get into the details of their past projects. Specifically, you want to see live websites that they've worked on, and case studies that lay out the kinds of challenges they've been able to address.

On the web design side, new clients tend to look at aesthetics and nothing else. If a website *looks* good, business people tend to assume that it must *be* good. When it comes to custom web programming, that kind of eyeball test just isn't good enough. While it's true that visuals matter (and we will discuss them in a moment), things like functionality, stability, and the long-term profitability of a project should be the decision criteria that matter most.

The best way to learn about your development team's experience in these areas is by taking some time with the case studies they offer. Here, you should be looking for projects that are similar to your own. You might not see clients in your same industry, but it's a good sign if you can find a few that have wanted to accomplish something that's similar to your ultimate goal. In other words, you want to know that your development team can program exactly what you're looking for.

Note, however, that most programmers are going to offer up their favorite clients and projects as samples and case studies (just like any of us would). These "wins" don't always tell you the whole story, though, which is why you need to dig a little bit deeper. I'll show you how to do that next.

Talk to Former Clients

You can learn a lot from case studies, but if you really want to find out what it's like to work with a web development company, talk to a few of their recent clients. In fact, if you have the opportunity, talk to a few clients who aren't mentioned in case studies or highlighted in portfolios.

You might be wondering what a former client can tell you that samples and detailed reports can't. That's easy: They can fill you in on how easy (or difficult) the development team was to work with, whether they were able to hit deadlines, if the work came in at or under budget, and how close they came to achieving the client's vision.

The more recently someone has worked with a programming team, the fresher their memories will be and the more insightful feedback you are likely to get. Web development companies know this, and should be happy to provide you with the contact details of a few people they have worked with in the last few months. If they can't or won't, you should take that as a bad sign.

To be sure you're getting all sides of the story, try to talk to a few different clients. Creative differences and other issues can make individual relationships difficult to manage and grow, but if several different former clients say something that gives you pause about working with the business, take that advice to heart.

Don't Forget the Design Aspect

Just a couple of pages ago, I told you to focus on the results of a web app project and not to fixate on the aesthetics. Now, I'm telling you that you need to scrutinize the design elements of an app before you choose a creative team. What gives?

All good web developers know that design and functionality go hand-in-hand. You can't make the most of one without the other. If a website looks great, but does nothing, then it's really just a pretty online brochure, isn't it? And on the other hand, if a website can do lots of amazing things, but is visually bland and cumbersome to use, then the brilliance of the concept is likely to be missed altogether.

Knowing this, you should pay special attention to the details of design within a development team's portfolio. You want to know that the web apps they've built have real power and have been valuable to the companies they were built for before anything else; after that, you want to be sure that things are presented in a way that's attractive, engaging, and user-friendly.

At this point, I could go into a pages-long rant about what does and doesn't make for good design, but the reality is you probably already know yourself. While it's not unusual for clients to have their own specific preferences, we all like clean lines, lots of white space, and easy-to-read fonts. Good design usually utilizes base colors that aren't repellent to normal people, and minimizes visuals that are gaudy, animated, and over-produced.

If you see designs you like, and that look natural and professional to you, then you know you're on the right track. On the other hand, if you see lots of great apps being buried within websites that are hard to look at, much less take seriously, then you might want to continue your search for a new vendor.

Feel Free to Shop Around

Although I haven't gotten into prices, fees, and payment terms yet, these will undoubtedly be big considerations in your mind as you consider various web development partners. We all have budgets to work within, and you certainly don't want to exceed yours (or bankrupt your company) when it's certainly not necessary to get good work.

I wish I could give you a good set of guide-lines to follow when it comes to fees for web app development, but as you might imagine, prices can be all over the board. Because there's no such thing as a "standard" web development project, there isn't really a standard fee you can count on, either. Variables like the experience of the team, the complexity of the project, where you're located, and how much time you have before your new website needs to launch all figure into the mix.

The best answer, then, is usually just to shop around. There's no need to be shy about this or hide it – a good web development partner won't just expect this, they'll encourage it. When someone steps into the offices of GoingClear Interactive, I want them to find the best fit for their needs and situations, even if that isn't with my company. We get plenty of business, and things work out better for everyone when the right match is made. You should choose a web programming team that feels the same way.

Along those same lines, keep in mind that it's easy to end up paying for someone else's prestige when choosing a web development company. To see what I mean, consider this: You make an appointment to meet with a potential vendor and arrive at their building, which is in a trendy downtown neighborhood. After taking an elevator to the top floor, you're greeted by an impossibly attractive person at the reception desk who steers you toward a number of gourmet coffee options and asks you to have a seat on a calfskin leather couch.

Once your appointment begins, you're astounded by the visual displays offered in an all-glass presentation room, with your meeting attended by several layers of creative and technical personnel. You leave with a colorful binder and proposal, stocked with dozens of pages of glossy charts and figures.

Is this kind of meeting impressive? Undoubtedly. But it's also going to be very, very *expensive*. All the money that it takes to lease that office space, buy that important furniture, and pay for those premium lattés has to come from somewhere, and it isn't just going to be the firm's *other* clients. Every hour of billable work you agree to contains quite a bit of overhead.

Granted, I'm a bit biased in this area, but at my company we run a pretty spartan ship. We put our clients first, but we rarely spend money on trivial, frivolous things (although to be fair, we *do* enjoy caramel-based coffee drinks). Despite the lack of official greeters, we turn out web apps and websites that stand up with any in the world. We just happen to do big agency work at a fraction of the price.

The question you have to ask yourself as a client is: How much is the glitz and glamour of working with a big web design agency worth to you? Do you want a great cup of coffee, or an affordable web app that helps your company grow?

Choose a Firm That Follows an Agile Approach to Development

Although I've told you most of what you need to know to choose the right web development company, there is one other factor you need to consider, even if it doesn't seem to make much sense to you now: *Choose a vendor that follows an agile approach to web development.*

If that doesn't seem like something that should be a priority for you, or you don't understand the concept, it's time to move on to the next chapter and see what the big deal is.

6 | Planning Your Web App

Once you have come up with a great web app concept that your development team can work with, can you sit back and wait for it to be delivered (in perfect working condition) in just a few days or weeks? Unfortunately, the answer is "probably not."

Although your development team will undoubtedly be doing the bulk of the work from here on out, there are still a few things you need to handle on your own… and some places where your guidance and feedback will be needed. Plus, it helps to have at least some working knowledge of what your vendor will be up to, just so you can hold on to the right kinds of expectations.

Over the next few chapters, I will walk you through various aspects of the web app development process that take place *after* you've established what it is you want designed or developed. Don't worry, we'll skip over most of the technical details and focus on the things that require your input or that matter to your business.

Getting to Know Your Design and Development Team

So far, we've been talking about your web programming team in the way that most clients tend to think of us: "as a group of people who are good with computers and websites."

That's a decent high-level description, but as we move into the project specification, wire-framing, and then development process, it can be helpful to have some idea of whom you're actually working with and what their different roles and tasks are. That way, you can better understand what's going on around you, and know where specific questions can be addressed.

Your main point of contact will likely be the project director. This person might have a different title, but they are essentially the one who's bringing everything together, communicating your needs to web designers and coders (although they will likely be involved in discovery meetings, as well), and generally ensuring that your project stays on track, on schedule, and on budget.

Working with and around them will be web designers, who are primarily concerned with aesthetics and user experience, web developers who actually write the code that makes your web software work, and potentially another group that will be responsible for technical details and quality assurance testing.

Depending on the size of a company – and even the size of your project – some of these jobs may overlap. It's not unusual for the owner of the business to be the lead project manager and creative director, while some web developers can be good at both coding and design. Likewise, lots of developers either do QA testing themselves or participate heavily in that process.

Having a sense of these different departments can give you a better mental picture of the next steps I'm going to walk you through. No matter what the specific titles and roles are, though, everyone should be on the same page and working to bring your web app concept to life.

Creating a Web App Project Specification Document

Before any actual web design or web development work on your web app begins, it's likely that your development team will work with you to put together a document called a "web app project specification document." You may hear these referred to by a shorter term: "web specs."

Don't let the name scare you. This doesn't necessarily have to be anything technical. Instead, it should be a list of everything your web app will do. Consider it a "wish list" for website functionality that you and your creative team will come up with.

At first, the web specs themselves can be loosely styled. In fact, we can rely largely on bullet points (like "the web app should automatically send emails to XYZ," or "the web app will then convert to the customer's local currency and check nearby warehouses"). The point here isn't to write beautiful prose, but to get across everything we can think of that you want your web app to do.

As you begin to write statements or bullet points with the help of your programming team, don't assume that anyone reading your web specs sheet will know anything about your company, or even the people who will be using the web app. Your development team will have addressed key issues and unique functionality with you during a discovery meeting, of course, but the point is to leave no stone unturned. When outlining the broad strokes of a web spec, it's better not to leave things to chance.

You've probably figured out already that the big mistake during this stage in the development process is to not be detailed enough. If we provide too much information, or give product specs that are redundant, then it might mean a few wasted minutes of reading. If we forget something that's important, though, your web app could end up not being as powerful or useful as it should be. That's a rare occurrence when working with a veteran development team like the one we have at GoingClear Interactive, but it doesn't mean we shouldn't take the time to add in as many details as possible.

Another tip is to remember that web specs aren't just about functionality, but also the interface. For example, if you want to see things styled a certain way, say so. As an example, you might indicate, "If the customer chooses a preferred delivery date that isn't possible, red text should be displayed saying..." Often, you'll discover details about what you want as you flesh out the web specs with your web development team. That's good, because the more details you can envision and establish early on, the easier it will be to deliver the end product you need.

A good way to add a lot of detail to your web specs – and flush out your own ideas and inspirations along the way – is to tell the story of a few average users. Give a short narrative that describes who they are, why they came to your website, and what they do at each interaction. How are they using your web app to get what they want? What things do you need to be sure to provide that will help them understand it and make the most from it?

Although you will likely be the driving, creative force behind the process of developing web specs, don't feel overwhelmed. The team you work with will have been through this process dozens of time before, if not hundreds, and can guide you through the relevant questions and issues that need to be addressed. What's important here is that you direct the process toward the finished web app you need. That means giving details and insights into the vision you have for the finished website and underlying web software.

In addition, some web app projects end up being inspired by a client, but advanced by the web development team because of time constraints or general preference. It just comes down to how involved you want to be – whether you want to be more hands-on or rely more on the experience and successes of your creative partner. Ultimately, it's your project and you make the final call. Just know that there are options in terms of how to approach web development and your involvement.

With this kind of information in hand, your web development team can turn around and create the first pieces of a wireframe. That's the first step in bringing your web app idea to life.

Wireframing

Wireframing essentially means that your web programming team (or other members of the team, like web designers or a creative director) will create an outline or blueprint for the web software they are going to fill in later.

Internally, building a wireframe usually begins with a "brain dump" that might not even take place inside a document or computer screen. I know from experience with my own firm that, depending on how simple or complex the web app is, and how many ideas we have, the first set of ideas might be scribbled down on sticky notes or scraps of paper. That way, they can be combined, rearranged, or put to one side without any fuss. Plus, doing things this way lets us add or take away thoughts without having to commit to anything while we are still playing around.

The wireframe essentially serves two purposes. The first is to serve as a collection of features, screens, tools, and interactions that all need to go into the web app. The second is to create a kind of flowchart we can use to envision the way the web app will look, which interactions will take place, how users can move from one screen, area, or feature to another, and so on.

This last point is particularly important. During the wireframing process, we will begin to assemble a roadmap that guides customers, employees, or other users through your website and within the app itself. Even if your web app is going to run in the background, or update itself automatically, it's important to think of when those interactions or updates will take place, where changes will be displayed, and how often they will occur, or under what specific set of events.

You could think of the wireframe for your web app as a flowchart, but in reality it's much more – it essentially becomes the spine of your web programming, supporting all the design, features, and coding that will take place later on.

In most cases, you can expect that your web development team is going to undergo the process of building a wireframe without your input. However, questions may come up during this stage, especially in regard to how you want various pieces of your web app to tie together, and what sorts of tools and functionality you need to offer to different users. Try to consider these issues carefully, because the answers you give will go a long way toward establishing what your web app will and won't do later on. At the same time, don't consider any answer at this stage to be final. I can tell you from past experience that the scope of your web app development project can change. Being flexible during the building process can be key to launching a successful web app.

Also, know that your vendor may show you different elements of the wireframe to ensure that what they're putting together meets your expectations. As you review the progress with them, remember that wireframes typically have very limited design. You may be shown mockups (see below) as part of the package, but whether you are shown these or not, evaluate the wireframe on the basis of functionality instead of design elements. Changing the look of a web app is relatively easy, especially during the design stage; adding new features or changing core functionality of what your users can do can be more challenging.

Screens and Aesthetics

At some point, usually during or after the wireframing process, your development team will start to put together mockups of different images, menus, and color schemes for you to review. Most likely they'll be static visuals, meaning that the graphics you see won't actually do anything. But they'll give you a sense of how your finished web app will look on your website, and the way the resulting interfaces will appear to users.

This is a step that most clients truly enjoy, if only because it finally seems as if their web app is actually coming to life. It's easier to envision the project as a real, finished business tool once you can see what it will look like.

While it can be tempting to give a quick "thumbs-up or thumbs-down" reaction to the design elements within your web app mockups, I would advise you to move beyond first impressions. Obviously, you have to like the look of your finished web app, so you should point out any issues or concerns you see. At the same time, though, remember to consider a few details, such as:

Does the proposed look of your web app match existing or future branding elements?

If it's going to be on your website, it should look like it belongs there. That's probably not an issue if you're getting web development in conjunction with an upgraded web design (something we'll explore in a coming chapter) — but if you're adding new functionality to existing pages, make sure everything integrates well.

Does the web app design meet the needs and expectations of the group that will be using it?

In other words, is it the right style for your customers, members, or employees? Finding a good answer to this question often means soliciting opinions from a few people who might not normally be involved in the decision-making process.

Does the design of your web app appear to be clean and straightforward?

Usability is a huge concern for any part of your website, and particularly with custom web programming. Having all the functionality in the world isn't helpful if users can't grasp things like menus and layout structures. It's easy for clients (and sometimes for their designers) to go overboard adding "glitz" to the way a particular page or item looks when something stripped down would actually be of more utility to the end user.

These are the kinds of questions you should have on your mind as you consider different elements of design that your web design team shows you. As you consider them, don't forget that functionality and aesthetics go hand-in-hand – if you pay all of your attention to one while ignoring the other, your web app isn't going to be as useful as it could be to your business, or to the men and women who are using it.

Avoiding Information Overload

It's not uncommon, somewhere through the planning, wireframing, and development process, for business people to become a little overwhelmed. There are so many variables and possibilities to manage that it all starts to look like an endless stream of numbers, ideas, and loose ends.

If you find yourself in that position, just remember this, courtesy of the GoingClear Interactive programming team: Developing a web app is really about managing the flow of information – where it's coming from, where it's going, how we're going to let users interact with it, and even how we want it to be presented. Figuring out the exact solutions requires a mixture of art, science, and even philosophy, but in its most basic sense it's just about making decisions and creating connections.

So long as you remember that it's a question of managing, steering, and presenting data, it's easy to take a step back from the minutia and see the bigger picture (not to mention the end benefit).

Streamlining Your Web App

UX, which is industry shorthand for "user experience," is a huge topic and a good reason to think about custom web development. Here is why: As your new website starts to take shape, you may begin to envision new tools or processes that would make it easier for buyers to get one page or concept closer to their end goal.

Streamlining UX can involve the creation of web apps that involve search, navigation, shopping carts, stored information, or even building dynamic hyperlinks (links that take users to different places based on the content they've seen, responses they've given, etc.).

Maximizing UX is best thought of as a process that's similar to what car and aircraft manufacturers use to reduce things like weight and drag. That is, you should remember that small changes made at key points can lead to incremental improvement. None of the gains might seem huge in the beginning, but put together, they add up to a website that *feels* easier to use and navigate. The more convenient and hassle-free it is for people to interact with your website, the more likely they are to stay on your pages and complete a transaction, fill in a form, or take whatever step you have defined as the business goal or revenue model for your web app.

Moving into the Design and Development Phase

It can be tempting to rush your web development team along and try to push them through the planning stage as quickly as possible. In fact, some programmers like to do exactly that and skip ahead past wireframing and initial designs (much less client meetings and phone calls) without much discussion or forethought.

Doing so is like having your cake before dinner. It's fun, but inevitably you just end up wishing you had done things differently when you had the chance.

As much as you are probably looking forward to seeing some new versions and releases of your web app, take the time to lay the groundwork for success in the beginning. Wireframes and design ideas are good (and important) starting points that speed up progress later, and a reputable web programming vendor won't move on until these have been finished. With the right background details set, your software will start to take shape quickly and you may see early releases much sooner than you would think.

But to ensure that things go smoothly from this step forward, you have to choose a web development partner with the right client-centered philosophy. That's something we'll address in the next chapter.

7 | Understanding the Agile Web Development Process

The chances are good that, as a business owner or executive, you imagine the web app development process to go something like this: You come up with a concept for a new piece of software, find a vendor who can design and code it (or work with your existing web design team to bring it to life), pay a fee, and then receive the finished product.

In a broad sense, things certainly work that way. However, somewhere along the line you'll likely have to make an important decision, and one that you may not know exists – the choice between a programming team that follows an agile approach to development, and one that goes by a standard or "waterfall" system.

We'll start with the second idea first, because it's the one most people are familiar with. In the waterfall approach to web development, you give your vendor a rough idea of what you want, and then they return with a proposal that includes all the "bells and whistles," complete with a project fee and a complete set of features. In other words, you know what you're getting upfront, and exactly what it's going to cost you.

In most parts of the business world, that's a good thing. But when it comes to web development – or *any* kind of web software programming – there's actually a better way. That better way is called "agile."

What Agile Development Is

To understand why agile web development is a superior option, and why I'm recommending you choose a firm that adheres to it, you first have to understand what it's all about.

That starts with an explanation that "agile" isn't a set system, procedure, or web software programming code. It's more like a philosophy – one that centers on getting the best possible results rather than sticking to rigid, predefined notions.

In a waterfall scheme, you essentially give your creative team a bit of money and then they come back to you with the finished product. Under the agile system, things work differently. They'll still collect the same basic data from you in the beginning, but instead of disappearing for weeks or months at a time, they'll engage in short bursts of activity working hard (and with few distractions) to provide you with something that's a good "first version" of your website or web app as quickly as possible.

Then, they'll bring that partially finished product back to you, explain what it can and can't do, and get your feedback. After they've received impressions from you and your team, and a little more direction, they'll start the same process all over again, adding to what's already been created with your most recent thoughts guiding them. In this way, you stay more connected to the process and have the option to make changes or improvements as you go along instead of being tied to your first set of ideas.

How Agile Development Actually Works

Let's take a closer look at how agile development actually plays out when you are having a web app programmed for your organization. Things begin just as you would probably expect they would with any vendor...

Step One: Meet, Discuss, and Gather Info

Good research is at the heart of any web design or web development project. You can't build something for a company until you understand what that company does, the challenges they face, and the end results they are hoping to achieve. You should never work with any vendor that doesn't place a high priority on the discovery phase of the creative process.

In web app development, this usually involves meeting with you and working collaboratively to develop a web app project specification sheet. Remember that your programmers are likely to ask a lot of questions. They know from experience that you probably have certain wants, needs, and assumptions that are in your mind but not necessarily clear to those who are on the outside looking in.

The information your development team gleans from this part of the process is critical, because it drives all the activity that's yet to come.

Another key point to remember about the discovery process is that no idea should be too wild, unconventional, or off the wall to consider. Sometimes, the right question, comment, or even "what if…" can be the game-changer that separates your web app from the rest, or takes your project to a whole new level. When you have a team full of creative minds and programming experts in a room, take advantage of it.

And finally, remember that "discovery" doesn't just happen at the beginning of the web app development process, but should be ongoing. You'll notice that we highlight the idea of working, developing, and then meeting together again to assess the results and future steps. This is critical. Email and phone calls are helpful for keeping a project on track, but nothing beats a good face-to-face strategy and brainstorming session once every week or two to foster creativity and imagine new solutions.

Step Two: Sprints of Activity

Those short, focused bursts of activity (which can last anywhere from a week to several weeks) are typically called "sprints." During a sprint, everyone is working together in a singular way to accomplish as much of the project as they possibly can. Things like email and cell phones go away, and programmers trade ideas – and sometimes go back and forth with client contacts – to get the most critical elements up and running.

Because everyone on your development team is working on a few prioritized items at a time, instead of checking things off a long list of features, the emphasis is on getting something that's finished and functional. That doesn't necessarily mean that your web app is going to be completed in this short amount of time, just that you're going to notice more progress than you probably would if you were simply waiting to hear back from your web development vendor at some future point in time.

Every sprint has a deadline, a firm ending point that marks a cutoff for current activity. As this draws closer, your development team will begin to tie things up to make the current version of your web app as complete, stable, and useful as possible.

Step Three: Review and Feedback

After a sprint has been completed, your development team will meet with you again and share the latest release of your web app. They'll show you how things are working so far, which features have been implemented, and how they've translated the web specs defined in the initial website planning phase.

More importantly, they'll give you a chance to review their progress so far and see what you like or don't like. This is a very big deal, and for a couple of reasons. First, if you see something in an early version of your web app that you don't like, there's plenty of time to make changes later. And second, it's surprisingly common for clients to realize at this stage that they would like their app to do things that they hadn't thought of during the initial brainstorming sessions.

In the traditional waterfall method of custom web programming, making large-scale changes to the direction the team is working in, or adding and subtracting features, would be a nightmare because you aren't going to see much of the web software until it's finished. With the agile approach, however, it's not such a big deal. All your creative team has to do is know what you'd like to see after the next round of activity, inform you of any changes to price and/or project fees that might apply, and then get back to work on a bigger version that incorporates any direction you are able to provide.

Step Four: Rinse and Repeat

After you've given your feedback, the next sprint can begin. You review each successive version of your web app, with each version being more functional and complete, and so on. The process continues, with sprints of various length, until your web app is complete and ready for testing.

The Benefits of the Agile Approach to Web Development

If you haven't worked with an agile development team in the past, know that it might feel a bit different when you get started. After all, it's more about the "best finished product" than it is a specific list of deliverables, and you're usually quoted a range of time and money instead of a set fee. That can feel uncomfortable, especially if you're going to be held responsible for any delays or cost overruns.

However, deciding to opt for agile development isn't akin to writing a blank check to your programming team (more on this in a second). And it always leads to better results.

There are numerous reasons why this is the case. The first has to do with the way things are managed within your vendor's team. Under an agile approach, everyone is working in a continuous and coordinated way during a sprint. That's not just energizing — it's a great way to remove distractions and get everyone's creative best.

Another benefit of the agile development approach is that it's collaborative and client-directed at the same time. Instead of simply paying your team to give you what they think is the best possible result, you're working right along with them to ensure that their execution matches your vision. You become a partner in the design and development process, with regular oversight of the project.

It would also be difficult to overstate how important it is that agile development is flexible. Regardless of what kind of programming team you opt to hire, it's a pretty sure bet that you're going to want to make changes to your web app somewhere along the way as it's being built. It's just something that happens all the time – clients get a look at a piece of web software and start thinking, "What if it could do..." and then things change in an instant. It's much better to plan for those eventualities ahead of time than it is to deal with them when you're trying to get your web app released.

And finally, you should know that going with a firm that follows an agile approach can save you time and money. For one thing, because you're not as firmly attached to a feature list like you would be under the waterfall approach, you aren't going to be penalized for switching gears or changing your mind on an important point. For another thing, clients often end up needing less time and programming than they think.

A moment ago, I admitted that business people always end up changing their web apps. What I didn't tell you is that the web apps don't always get bigger or more complicated. Sometimes, clients are so pleased by what they've seen after a sprint that they decide to tie up a few loose ends and call it "finished." We might find simpler ways to achieve the end result they were looking for, or decide to do away with a feature that ends up being redundant. In each case, the client gets exactly what they needed and were looking for, but faster and for a smaller budget than they anticipated.

As I've said, agile web development isn't just a programming or project management strategy; it's a philosophy that centers on getting clients what they want and need in the fastest, most efficient way possible. That makes it the best choice for most web development projects.

Like anything in life, though, there are exceptions to the rule. Suppose, for example, that your web development project is very straightforward, or that you already have a list of defined features you need (perhaps because you've gotten your inspiration elsewhere, or started your project with one web development company and are now taking it to another). Or it might be the case that to get approval for your programming project, you need a specific budget and timeline to stick to.

In these cases, the traditional approach might be better, and could work wonderfully. Never forget that this process is all about getting you the best web app possible, not adhering to any one style or philosophy. Most of the time, using agile development is going to be your most efficient and cost-effective choice. But don't let that ruin your inspiration if you have constraints that make agile development impossible.

8 | Launching Your Web App

Once your web app has been developed and integrated into your website, it's time to get things ready for your launch. Depending on the complexity of the web programming project, and whether you have an existing website already, this can be a very big step or a barely noticeable one.

Either way, there are essentially three steps to launching a new web app: Testing the build, getting the word out, and then performing any follow-ups or maintenance.

It would be nice if we could finish programming a web app, put it into place, and then flip a switch that suddenly turned it on and made it active on the Internet. Unfortunately, that's not the way things work, and web development firms that follow anything resembling this approach (and there are a few out there) are just asking for trouble.

Here is why: The very worst thing that can happen to your website isn't a delay in its launch, but the release of a finished product that isn't quite finished. Throw something that isn't polished or functional online, and bad things are going to happen. In a matter of days, or maybe hours, you're going to discover that it doesn't appear correctly (or at all) in certain browsers, that it doesn't link to the databases or information feeds it's supposed to at certain times, or that it doesn't work at all for certain segments of your customer base.

Those problems are bad enough, but things get even worse if you have issues of security or compatibility that cause other applications to crash. Once that happens, you can bet that users are going to start expressing their dissatisfaction – not just to you, but also with each other. And once negative reviews and bad word-of-mouth start spreading, your business is in real trouble, regardless of how strong your original concept was.

To avoid those kinds of outcomes, reputable web development companies like mine do lots of rigorous quality assurance testing before a web app ever goes live. In particular, this involves installing the web pages or web software on a dedicated server, offline, and essentially "pretending" that it's on the Internet to see how it reacts to certain requests or situations. We'll access it via different browsers and computers, see whether it can function effectively on our test server with multiple people trying to use it once, and even make a few attempts at "hacking" your web app to make sure it can stand up to online attacks.

In addition, your web developer may encourage you to play with this version of your web app, as well, and to invite your family, friends, and colleagues to test it out with you. Because we don't know what they are trying to accomplish, and may use the web app differently than we would, they make excellent beta testers. Also, it's not unusual for clients to think of one last feature or idea they want to add to their web app at this stage. Those little last-minute adjustments can mean the difference between something that's merely functional and a website that's outstanding.

Despite what exactly turns up, finding bugs during this stage of the process, and not after your web app has gone live, is priceless. This is mainly due to the fact that you can always find two types of web developers in this world: those who occasionally make mistakes and the others who are filthy liars. What I'm getting at is that something might have been overlooked or might need more attention, no matter how talented and diligent your programming team is.

Aside from the kinds of hands-on testing I referred to a moment ago, most web quality assurance work will take place behind the scenes within your development team's offices. So why bother mentioning it at all?

There are two big reasons: knowledge and timing. In the first case, you don't have to know how to test your web apps, but you *do* need to know that someone is testing them, and doing a good job of it, on your behalf. Make sure any programming company you hire has a thorough and rigorous plan in place to make sure that your web app is going to work exactly the way it's supposed to.

The second issue has to do with time. As you approach the end of your agile web development cycle, your vendor will likely include a small chunk of billable time for these activities. Occasionally, clients try to fight this, or push us to rush through the testing process because "everything seems fine." Don't settle for something that's 95% finished when the extra touches could make or break your business, not to mention allow security risks to go unnoticed.

Web app testing is a crucial part of the job, and one that you and your development partner should appreciate the value of.

Spreading the Word About Your Web App

Few things are quite as depressing as spending weeks or months building a truly spectacular web app and then watching it go unused. It's the kind of wasted effort that makes web programmers groan out loud; I can't even imagine how painful it would be for a paying client.

Usually, when a web app goes unused – or a website unvisited – it's because not enough thought is put into the marketing and promotion of the finished product. It's simply not enough, in this day and age where hundreds or thousands of competitors are a click away, to put something online and hope the people you want to find it will come and start using it. They *might*, and your new web app could go viral and attract its own visits… but that's not a plan I'd rely on, no matter how strong your concept is.

Instead, you need to promote your new web app as if it were a groundbreaking combination of art and technology (which it might well be). You need to make sure that your best potential customers or members don't just hear about your launch, but hear about it several times and in several ways. Here are just a few of the tools you can use to make that happen:

Email marketing – Assuming you have a good list of customers or interested subscribers, there is no cheaper, faster, or more effective way to get the word out on your new website – or upgraded website with new custom web programming features – than through email marketing. In fact, if you don't have a targeted list to use, you might consider renting one or pursuing affiliate partnerships for a major launch or update.

Search engine optimization – Did you know that Google currently processes more than 2 billion search queries per day? It's a good bet that at least some of those people, and probably thousands of them, are looking for exactly what your web app offers. Search engine optimization is a big topic, but it basically boils down to adding well-researched keywords to page titles, headings, and different relevant areas of your website while getting other credible websites to link to yours. Making just a few of these changes can increase your web visibility and bring lots of traffic your way.

Social media updates – If Google's search engine is still top dog on the web, then social media websites like Facebook, Twitter, and LinkedIn can be equally as important. By using teasers, announcements, and even specialty forums or groups, you can take advantage of pre-existing social media audiences to draw visitors to your website during a new launch, especially if you have specials or promotions to offer.

Bloggers and reviews – Does the market you want to serve have influential bloggers, reviewers, or websites that fans or customers frequent? If so, sending them notices well in advance of your launch or update could be a great way to leverage their readership and garner some attention for your new web app. Often, a quick Google search is all that's needed to discover dozens of different people and outlets who would be interested in hearing about your new venture.

Video marketing – YouTube has been called "the second most popular search engine," after Google, because it gathers billions of hits per month from people looking for lifestyle and career tips, how-to guides, and product reviews. Promoting your new web app with an online clip – posted to YouTube and elsewhere – could be an inexpensive way to draw lots of new potential customers to your concept.

Internet advertising – Advertising costs money, but it also works quickly and effectively, and can be used to get your new web app in front of specific groups of buyers at exactly the right time. From pay-per-click search ads to sponsored social messages and ads directed to specialized industry or topic websites, the possibilities for finding new customers are virtually endless. And contrary to popular belief, Internet advertising doesn't always require big budgets. You'd be amazed at the amount of targeted traffic you can generate to your website for a few cents per visitor.

Press coverage – With all the attention that's paid to Internet marketing these days, it's easy to forget that traditional media outlets (like television, radio, and even newspapers) still have large audiences that can be convinced to give your web app a try. Plus, media companies have websites that draw lots of visitors, too, giving you valuable links and exposure that could help turn your web app into a success.

Offline marketing – Depending on your business model, you may be able to use direct mail, flyers, and even offline print or telephone advertising to generate interest in a new web app.

One observation I've made over many years in the Internet digital marketing industry is that momentum is a powerful thing, especially just after the launch of a new web app or website. When people are excited about trying something, and sharing information about it, the news can take on an almost viral effect, with a company's contacts sharing details with *their* contacts, and so on. It doesn't take much for a spark of interest to become a wildfire of activity.

Of course, the inverse is also true. When something new arrives on the Internet and is met with collective silence, or the virtual equivalent of crickets and tumbleweeds, it's hard to generate a lot of enthusiasm after the fact. This is partly because things are more exciting when they're new, and partly because failures become self-fulfilling – if it seems like no one is interested in a new launch, it's only natural for the creators or entrepreneurs behind it to turn their attention elsewhere.

Launching a new web app is a huge achievement, and one that probably has significance to your customers and those interested in your topic or industry. Make sure to use every tool at your disposal to get the word out, spread awareness, and make an early impact in the market. Those first early efforts at promotion can go a long way toward making your company or project successful later.

Taking the Next Steps

A lot of amazing things can start to happen once your web app has been launched. In some cases, the bottom-line effects can be immediate, with new sales coming in virtually overnight. In other instances, it may take a while for customers, employees, or colleagues to catch on.

Either way, you never want to think of your web app as being "finished," even after it's been tested and launched. There's always room to grow and more to try. Coming up with a great idea and seeing it turned into something people can use is a great first step; building on that success by expanding your web app, adding new features, and streamlining the user interface is necessary if you want to keep from falling behind competitors who want to copy your success.

Your web app, and your website as a whole, should always be improving. In the next chapter, we're going to look at what you can do to refine your web app over time and keep making your business stronger.

9 | Refining Your Web App

Try as you might, you will probably never launch a perfect web app. There will always be another feature you'd like to add, a bug that needs to be resolved, or an assumption that proves to be incorrect.

And even if you could develop and launch a web app with no flaws, it would quickly become outdated. The market would change, competitors would catch up, and technology would advance to the point where something new will possibly replace what you have already launched. Remember, iron tools were once cutting edge.

The takeaway here isn't that striving for excellence is futile, but that even the very best web app development projects should be in a constant state of refinement. No matter how well your website and company are doing, there are always areas for improvement and you should seek to find them. And if things *aren't* going well, that's all the more reason to go into problem-solving mode.

Don't take a "launch and forget" attitude toward web app development. Do everything you can to make sure that the best possible build and version are available for your customers, employees, and users, but don't be afraid to go back to the drawing board and see if you can come up with even better ideas later on. The minute you become complacent, you start falling behind, and continual excellence brings continual profit opportunities.

In this chapter, we're going to take a very brief look at a few of the reasons you might want to update and refine your web apps after they've been launched.

Dealing with Unexpected Problems

In most cases, a good web development team is going to work out technical "bugs" and compatibility issues long before your web app ever goes live. In the rare event that something does go wrong in one of these areas, they should be happy to fix it for you as quickly as possible. In fact, a good web development team will have built in a warranty for a set period of time in which they'll correct any problems for free after your official launch.

The kinds of unexpected events that cause problems with web apps aren't due to programming, however, but outside issues and influences. For example, a website built around weather reports can't function if those reports don't arrive automatically or aren't accurate. An e-commerce shopping tool might fail if prices aren't being converted from one currency to another following a major economic event.

The list of things that can go wrong with a web app, and a business in general, is virtually endless. That's what makes planning for the unexpected such an impossible exercise – you can think about areas of concern, but there's just no telling what sorts of challenges are going to creep up in the future.

In most cases, the "why" of your web app problem isn't all that important; finding a solution is. This is where those qualities you should be looking for in a development team – like experience, creativity, and a client-friendly philosophy of business – come into play. You want a team that can come up with imaginative solutions and put them into place quickly.

It takes a lot of time and effort to develop a web app and grow a successful company. Don't let your profitable idea slip away just because you run into an unanticipated roadblock.

Responding to User Feedback

Just as you can't predict what's going to happen in life or business, it's not always possible to know how people are going to react to your new web app, either… or which new features they'll ask for in the future.

The good news is that successful online businesses are largely driven by user feedback – when people take the time to tell you what they like or want, it's usually because they intend to keep buying from you in the future. So if you find yourself getting lots of requests for a new feature, or complaints about something you don't offer with your existing web app, take it as a positive development (even if it doesn't seem like one at the moment).

Additionally, the more your business and web platform and grow, the farther you should go to actively solicit opinions from buyers, colleagues, and vendors. Even if you know you have a core business model that works, it's never a bad idea to find out if there are more "extra touches" you can integrate into your web presence that would be useful to them, or make working with you more convenient.

Remember that success in any business is largely about keeping the customers you have, and that existing buyers tend to place bigger orders, purchase your products and services more often, and cost you less money than new customers do. Ask for their opinions and take them seriously. Responding to user feedback, especially the kinds of suggestions you hear again and again, is a great way to ensure future revenue will keep coming in.

Studying the Competition

Watching your competitors is an interesting part of the web development process. In theory, everything you do should be based on your own strengths, and your customers' needs, with a sense of disregard for whatever other business owners and marketers might be doing. In reality, though, we all know it's good practice to keep an eye on those who would like to see your business fail, and you can expect they'll be watching you, as well.

In a lot of situations, that means your web development projects are likely to be emulated by others in your industry, and often more quickly than you might expect. The second you begin doing something innovative, you can bet one of your competitors is going to start wondering whether they could do it too (or worrying about what will happen if they don't). This can be annoying – but it's usually a sign that you just have to keep following the improvement and refinement process I'm suggesting in this chapter.

(Besides, there's a silver lining here: You've become the trendsetter in the market, and have others responding to your moves. That's always a good thing.)

On the other hand, what happens when a competitor copies your web app and improves upon it? Or worse, comes out with something new and market-changing out of the blue?

The first step is to take a deep breath and stay calm. Keep in mind what I reminded you about earlier: Customers choose their vendors for a lot of different reasons, and even in very crowded, ultra-competitive markets, there is room for lots of different businesses to succeed.

Beyond that, the best thing to do is study the web app and see whether or not it's *really* better than what you've got on your website. Keep in mind that your competitor may have just burned through a huge part of their budget to get a very temporary bump in interest, which may quickly fade. Often, new pieces of web software seem groundbreaking, but offer little more than a fresh look or over-complicated features. And if it *is* actually superior, then you'll have to decide whether to react to the new web app, emulate some of its features into your own website, or take the next step to find a way to surpass it.

Most of the time, that's the best course of action. Competition is good for consumers, but it's also good for us as business owners, executives, and marketers. If someone else in your industry is pushing the limits, don't get mad, be thankful… and then start brainstorming ways to release something they won't be able to keep up with.

Improving User Experience

What your web app *does* is important, as is its stability. If it's not easy to use, though, it's never going to be as efficient or successful as it could be.

For that reason, some of the best (and most important) refinements you can make to your web app are in the area of user experience. This includes things like improving the aesthetics, streamlining the flow of traffic from one point on your website to another, giving more search options, and adding things like better menus and instructions.

Sometimes, UX can be improved simply by listening to customer feedback or studying web analytics packages. That's particularly true if you see users leaving your website at a certain point, or entering related terms into internal search dialogue prompts again and again.

This is an area of business and web development where you can earn style points, so don't overlook the value in improving UX as you continue to upgrade your web app in the future.

Expanding to New Features

Sometimes, the best ideas for expanding your web app come just like your original inspiration did – with a bit of brainstorming or an "aha" moment.

These kinds of epiphanies can be hard to manufacture, of course, but the better you get at keeping an open mind, and listening to your customers and competitors, the more often they'll come to you. Not every idea is going to be a winner, but you should never dismiss a new thought out of hand simply because it seems ambitious or far-fetched, either.

The best web apps are always growing, and the most successful companies in the world are always taking on new challenges. Look at a few major corporations and you'll see just what I mean: A lot of the world's biggest organizations started out selling products or solving problems that no longer exist in the modern world.

From time to time, make an appointment with yourself – or better yet, members of your staff and your web development team – to go over the progress of your web app and discuss future opportunities. The next feature you come up with could be the one that catapults your business into a new level of profitability.

10 | Bringing It All Together: 5 Real-Life Web Apps

Now that you know a bit about web apps and what they can do, let's look at a few ways companies are using them to improve efficiency and increase profits in the real world.

Below, you'll find brief descriptions of five web development projects that were produced by myself and my team at GoingClear Interactive. I didn't choose these to promote my own business – or at least not only to promote my own business – but because I know the backstory associated with each project and can speak to the different outcomes that were achieved.

Beyond that, each one represents a different kind of approach to programming, complete with its own audience and revenue model. It's likely that you might see elements of your own business or entrepreneurial idea in more than one of them. As you read through each one, think of how the tools being used could be applied to your situation, even if you work in a completely different industry.

OrganicRestaurants.com

More and more, diners around the country are looking for organic foods for themselves and their families. Concerns about pesticides, additives, and GMOs are increasingly common, but finding organic eateries can be a hit-or miss proposition, especially if you're traveling or are looking into organic dining for the first time.

That's where organicrestaurants.com comes in. As a large-scale worldwide directory for restaurants that serve organic food, it offers localized results and listings for this specialty business category.

What makes organicrestaurants.com such a great web app is that it isn't just a one-of-a-kind resource, but also a platform that's incredibly easy for users and businesses to take advantage of. For diners, locating organic eateries in a certain area is as simple as typing in a city name or ZIP Code. In seconds, they can see a variety of restaurants that offer just what they're looking for. They can even see the reviews that previous customers have left, mark restaurants as favorites, and contribute feedback themselves.

For restaurant owners and managers, on the other hand, adding information, uploading menus, refining their listing and viewing listing statistics (such as where their viewers are coming from and what they clicked on) is a snap. By registering their listing (or claiming it if it already exists on the site), they can even elect to sponsor their listing through a premium placement opportunity, guaranteeing a top placement on the specific city results page of where their listing is located or in a neighboring city as well.

With a simple and secure four-step checkout system, advertising via premium placement on the site is a no-brainer decision for most restaurant owners who want to promote their businesses cost-effectively. And a clean user-friendly layout with lots of photos makes the web app easy for even first-time visitors to take advantage of.

This project is a great example of what can happen when you take a personal passion or interest and combine it with a proven, advertising-based revenue model. Specialized directories mean solid business opportunities. Could you launch the next one?

UniversalDentalPlan.com

This web app took an existing business model and made it better. Around the country, there are lots of dental savings plans available as a substitute or replacement for employer-provided dental insurance. Consumers pay a monthly fee, and get access to the same discounts and savings as they would if they were insured, provided they go to participating dentists.

The owners of this website came to us with an insightful question: what would happen if they took their entire framework and moved it online?

The result is a robust web app that has numerous features for patients and providers alike. For those needing dental care, there are options to register on the website and log in to manage subscriptions, schedule appointments, and see the details of different providers in the area. Dental offices can advertise their services, update their profiles, and take advantage of built-in CRM systems that manage leads and patient contact information.

Because dentists already buy into the dental savings plan on a subscription basis, monetizing this web app was a simple matter of integrating the service into existing monthly and yearly fees.

Although there are several similar web apps and other industries, we have yet to find another that is specifically tailored to dental professionals and their specific needs. As a result, this platform – and the underlying company – continues to gain in popularity and offers practitioners a way to increase billing while avoiding redundant communications and paperwork.

The Cask 'n Flagon

When this world famous pub came to us to talk about web development, we knew it wouldn't be because they needed help with online marketing. Sitting adjacent to Fenway Park, the landmark establishment serves cold beers and good times to thousands of guests every day, and is frequently filled to the point of being "standing room only."

What we learned during our initial meeting was that the owners of The Cask 'n Flagon were thinking ahead and looking for smarter ways to manage their employees. They wanted an intranet that could be accessed by their staff from anywhere, and that could automate a number of tasks that were taking up too much time and money.

Before long, we had built them a new web app that was available only to employees through a log-in portal. Once inside, team members could receive training, see (and change) work schedules, fill out required employment paperwork, and even arrange for things like direct deposits and employment benefits.

This is another case where simple pieces of technology were combined into web apps that let everyone win. The employer saves time and money every month, and team members get the flexibility to manage schedules, payments, and other human resource details from anywhere. The resulting automation means more money, improved convenience, and fewer hassles for everyone.

Custom web programming doesn't always have to be about reaching out to new customers, installing CRM systems, or generating revenue through e-commerce. Saving money in your company is just as good as earning it, and automating mundane HR and management tasks with secure web programming on an internal server is a great way to make everything smoother while padding your bottom line.

TrainingOnDemand.tv

While training is vital to teach new employees the specifics of their job and create opportunities for existing staff to expand knowledge and sharpen skills, it is often a time-consuming and expensive endeavor. The founders of TrainingOnDemand. tvTM knew there had to be a better way to provide timely, consistent training in a manner that is more efficient and cost-effective and set out to develop an eLearning website to meet this critical need.

The resulting platform is equal parts intuitive and powerful: it gives TrainingOnDemand.tvTM clients a way to upload training documents, videos, and courses so they may be accessed by learners 24 hours a day, 7 days a week in the office or in the comfort of their own home. The incorporation of timed tests ensures learning objectives are achieved. The availability of continuing education credit creates tremendous value for a variety of professional disciplines.

The model for the TrainingOnDemand.
tvTM website is simple. Clients, pay an annual
hosting fee for a branded eLearning website
which includes a live Help Desk for users.
TrainingOnDemand.tvTM staff work with client
subject matter experts to create training modules
and provide production support services for an
added cost. Clients choose which materials or
courses to upload, decide when to offer access to
individual employees, and can track progress in
real-time.

TrainingOnDemand.tvTM identified a need in
the marketplace and met it through the smart use
of digital automation. The TrainingOnDemand.
tvTM website is quickly growing as a training
resource for human service professionals with
customers loving its ease and convenience.

Houghton Mifflin Harcourt Sales Enablement Team

Every company needs new sales to grow. And to
find new customers, businesses need their sales
teams to be educated and equipped with up-to-
date product knowledge and details.

For the Sales Enablement group at Houghton Mifflin Harcourt (HMH), that was proving to be a challenge. They had approximately 800 reps spread across the United States, supported by online training programs being offered throughout the year. In order to take them, sales personnel were forced to register using Microsoft Excel files that were emailed and updated manually by another member of the HMH staff. The spreadsheets themselves were extremely cumbersome, with hundreds of rows and columns that needed to be filled in one at a time.

This spreadsheet-based system was functional, but it was prone to errors and didn't represent a valuable use of the Sales Enablement team's time and resources. Eventually, they turned to GoingClear Interactive for help developing a web app that would automate these tasks. The company was on a tight deadline ahead of its next training initiative, but wanted to work with a firm who would focus on intensive discovery and custom programming with the goal of finding a more efficient solution.

After thorough interviews and detailed planning, our experienced programmers were able to develop a successful web app that removed the need to share spreadsheet files through email. Instead, HMH got a streamlined solution that allowed for users to login, select the courses they needed, and have them automatically scheduled or assigned.

By giving HMH a new way to handle sales rep training, we didn't just eliminate an annoyance… we let their talented employees get back to what they did best – putting their focus back on more exciting, revenue-generating work.

Is Your Success Story The Next One?

These quick success stories should give you a little bit of real-world insight into the different ways web apps can be used to build a stronger, more efficient business. The real question isn't how others did it, though, but whether you're ready to step forward and turn your ideas into realities.

Before we conclude this book, I want to challenge you to get started on your web app development project, and to give you a couple of final points to think about. So, stay with me and read on for just a few more pages…

Conclusion

Conclusion: Are You Ready to Build Your Web App?

Now that we are reaching the end of this book, I hope I've convinced you that web development really isn't all that intimidating, and that web apps – pieces of software that automate business tasks – can transform entire organizations and industries.

On its own, a bit of code can save your business untold amounts of time and money. Put together, they can help you achieve game-changing results in thousands of different ways.

The truth is, I want you to build a web app because there is so much you can do with them, and so many places your company can go. However, there is a word of caution that I have to issue before you get started.

The Truth About Creating and Launching a Web App

As you've probably noticed, I'm very much in favor of web app development. However, it would be fair to say that it's not for everyone, or every situation. For new companies, hard work, research, and promotion *must* be important priorities.

Contrary to what some vendors might have you believe, custom programming is not a get-rich-quick scheme. There are some companies that launch web apps and thrive almost immediately, and with very little effort. For every one of them, though, there are a dozen others who had a really fantastic concept and either couldn't see it through or wouldn't do the hard work of promoting their creation.

On the Internet, ambitious and well-funded competitors are everywhere. As a startup or business with a new web app to promote, you can overtake them and carve out your market or niche, but you're going to have to fight for every inch... especially at first.

If you simply launch your web app and hope for others to find it or respond, you're likely to be disappointed. It takes a bit of work, and more than a little bit of creativity, to get off the ground and running.

In this book, I've been encouraging you to think carefully about whether you have a great idea for a web app. Now, here at the end, it's time to add a second question: Are you willing to do the work to ensure that it's successful?

If you are, then you have the only two ingredients that are necessary for success. If not, you're likely to end up being disappointed no matter how strong your concept is. Remember: A good web development team can build a great web app for you — but it's up to you to work the marketing plan you've developed with your creative team and bring it to the market and find your users or customers.

Of course, established businesses – and especially those launching web apps that will be internally used and managed – don't have to face some of these challenges. Depending on what kind of network and support you already have in place, launching a successful web app could be as simple as sending out a few emails to employees. I can't tell you how easy or difficult it's going to be, only that you need to plan for what happens after your web app is launched, not just for its development.

It really comes down to this: There are plenty of web apps already out there – some that have become a part of the daily lives of millions, and some that never even saw the light of the day. If you *are* going to build your web app, then do everything you can to focus on falling into that first group. Focus on making your project great, and not just another web app with a nice look and poor functionality. Work to develop your idea to its fullest potential, and then have a plan to let the world know about it.

Looking Ahead to the Possibilities

Every day, each of us uses products and technologies that might have seemed like science fiction just 10 years ago. Now, they are so ingrained into our lives that we couldn't imagine living or working without them. The next innovation could be yours. That realization, all by itself, should be all the motivation you need to get excited about having someone develop a web app on your behalf, whether you have a brand-new startup idea, or a part of your existing business that you want to automate and leverage through web programming.

Every year, people just like you and me redefine industries, create business empires, and change the way things are done simply because they ask "what if?" and decide to follow the answer to see where it leads. Who is to say that your web app idea won't be the first link in a chain that ends with something revolutionary? And even if it isn't, could it still be worth a try?

Even if you don't earn millions or billions of dollars from your project, it could help change lives, or spur new innovation, just because you decided to act on inspiration or impulse. Don't let the idea of a little bit of hard work and promotion scare you – with the right marketing plan, and a little bit of dedication, your new web app will bring you closer to your goal of getting more traffic and more users while continually refining itself into a finely tuned automated or revenue-creating machine!

Web app development is accessible and affordable. More than that, though, it *works*. Are you ready to jump in and get started?

Paul J. Scott is the founder and president of GoingClear Interactive, a Boston-based web design and web development firm.

Entrepreneurial from a young age, Paul got his "big break" in the business world caddying for influential business leaders as a teenager in Nantucket. He carried the lessons learned from those encounters into the corporate world, where he got his professional start managing websites and advertising for a large publishing company.

In 2001, Paul decided to launch his own business, GoingClear Interactive, by working evenings and weekends in a shared studio space. A focus on creative thinking, client service, and commonsense solutions helped to grow the company quickly, and the firm is now considered a leader in custom web development. Today, GoingClear Interactive works with businesses, nonprofits, universities, and government agencies of all sizes, helping them to make the most of web programming and their websites.

A Boston native, Paul is a graduate of Bentley University and holds a master's certificate in web development and e-commerce from Clark University. When he's not finding new ways to make websites work, he enjoys spending time with his family, motorcycling, learning, yoga, training in Krav Maga, volunteering for the Big Brothers program, golfing, and other activities.

You can learn more about Paul and his company GoingClear Interactive at GoingClear.com.

www.ingramcontent.com/pod-product-compliance
Lightning Source LLC
Chambersburg PA
CBHW072310210326
41519CB00057B/3978